MW01119063

Enjoy.

- Proverbs 3:15

She is more precious than rubies, and
nothing you desire can compare with her.

The
Bible.

\- Imam Ali (AS)

Women are like flowers, they must be treated gently, kindly, and with affection.

The Quran.

- Manusmriti 3.55-3.56

Women must be honored and adorned and where women are revered, there the gods rejoice.

The Veda.

Thee' Introduction

This book was written in honour of the women who still dream about experiencing that soft love, that grow-old-together love, that fairy tale love. Although, yes, no relationship is ever perfect, the following lessons are principles I've adapted to keep myself safe from toxic situations. We can't control how we are treated but we can control what we tolerate and it all starts with you.

Half self help book, Half self-development book.

Leanne 💗

Contents page

Lesson 1 - The subtle beauty of detachment

The root of suffering

is attachment.

Detachment simply means that you're able to leave as soon as you're not being treated how you desire to be treated. Mastering detachment gives you a filthy amount of power because you're less likely to fall victim to unhealthy 'soul ties' or obsessive levels of 'attachment' because you will never invest your emotions in a situation **until** your partner totally satisfies all of your needs, wants, and expectations.

Being able to detach yourself from a situation that your mind, body, and soul are deeply invested in may seem mission impossible and oftentimes we'd rather accept less in exchange for a person's intimacy, company or conversation...just as long as we get to keep them around. The thing is, as soon as you settle, you'll start to be accustomed to someone's poor treatment and you'll subliminally set your standards low. The only way to preserve your peace is by leaving when things turn toxic.

There are multiple ways to detach & let go of someone; it's up to each individual to figure out what works best for them.

- Some people believe in the concept of "outta sight outta mind" meaning as long as you can't see or speak to them, you will gradually move on and detach.
- Some people need to practice self-love and find themselves in order to realise that moving on would be the best thing for them now that they are aware of their value.
- Some people just need to find a distraction, like the gym, and let time take its course.
- Some people need to burn all the memories attached to the situation like the clothes, pictures, and gifts.
- Some people need to get even
- & some people need to do all of the above (me) ;)

Which one works for you?

_____

The two main types of attachments are...

Physical & Emotional attachments.

A **physical** attachment is often labeled as a 'soul tie' and this is when your body craves the person's touch and intimacy. You feel most loved and safe when you are in their arms and the sensation you endure when they give you intimacy is a feeling you rely on and become addicted to.

Can you break a physical attachment?

The simple answer is yes. The main way I believe you can break this attachment is to practice distance, and allow your body to adapt to life without their touch. Reintroduce your body to life as it was before you let them in and sooner or later, your body won't crave or remember the satisfaction you felt from their touch. Physical attachments are like a drug, their love and touch will always be a sensational feeling yet that same touch might be the reason you'll need healing.

An **emotional** attachment is much deeper and harder to break. This is when your partner plays a significant role in your mental and emotional well-being. Your own personal happiness will be solely dependent on their actions towards you. Emotional attachments are scary because they can make you naive as it will become hard to differentiate the tough and rough reality vs your own made-up perception of the person.

Can you break an emotional attachment?

I'll admit ...it's hard. I could say pray, fast, and meditate, but it is hard because you can't ever really force yourself to stop feeling the way you do. The best advice is to let time do its thing. The moment you truly believe that there is better out there for you... is the moment you will detach.

Emotional attachments are odd because when you're with that person you're at peace and without them, you're in pieces yet also, with them you're in pieces and without them, you're at peace.   It's weird.

Things to remember about detachment.

"Detachment is the ability to enjoy someone while being open to the probability of losing them"

"If your presence is not appreciated, make them feel your absence"

"Learn to leave the table when love, kindness, and admiration are no longer being served"

"Someone who loves you won't put themselves in a position where they can lose you"

"A Deep attachment to someone unhealthy will enslave you to them"

_What's your favorite quote and why:

_____

Lesson 2 - Do not, I repeat, Do not be the ride or die...

You will die.

Ride or die (in this case) is a term used to describe a woman constantly willing to stick with their partner even in the face of betrayal. I used to think that being the main chick & the one that has been by his side the longest was an accomplishment, that it meant something deep. Until I had an auntie (Big up Lisah) who told me "The one who is made a wife and still gets mistreated is not the winner but is instead the queen of the idiots and she's no better than a side chick" and that stuck with me forever.

Don't let men convince you that cheating, ghosting, or just plain disrespect is a part of a couple's "ups & downs" because it's not. No relationship is perfect, yes, but it is 100% possible to date someone who wouldn't dare disrespect you or leave you in emotional distress on purpose. The more a guy does you wrong & you take him back...the less both of you will respect the entire situation and that's when the toxicity starts.

Men do not respect the ride or dies, they use them as a safe space because they know you'll always hold it down. So there's no point bragging that "he always comes back" but instead ask yourself, why does he feel so comfortable to come back, Why do I always take him back and why am I in this vicious cycle?

Maturing will make you realise that men are slightly more emotionally intelligent than we think because the majority of the time they know what they want from the jump. That's why I emphasise that being a ride or die isn't worth it because, in the end, he will find a woman that he deems worthy enough to change for.

Ladies also remember that you can be the most independent, intelligent, Beautiful, and overall amazing woman but that doesn't mean you are his "Dream wife" Sometimes men dream of having a less emotionally intelligent woman so that he can have his ego fed for breakfast, lunch, and dinner hence why men still cheat on the most genuine ladies. Most of the time it's not you, it's him.

Things to remember about letting go.

"Sometimes the good you see in someone doesn't even really exist"

"You can be the whole package and more but if delivered to the wrong address, they won't know what to do with you"

"Let go of what you can't change"

"If the situation is Godsent, cheating and abuse are out of the equation because God knows you deserve the best"

"Don't think that the same person who broke your heart is going to be the one to fix it"

Lesson 3 - "Someone" vs "The one'

There's a difference.

Learn it

In our lifetimes we are going to come across so many people who we momentarily believe are 'the one' but they're really not and being able to differentiate when a guy is "the one" or just a "someone" is a hard but essential skill to master.

What's the difference?

Somebody who's a 'someone' is often put in your life to teach you a few lessons, give you some new experiences and overall just fill the current void of loneliness but it's key to remember that they're there for the moment, whether it's a couple of weeks, months or even a few years, they're not your person and you aren't theirs. Prepare to come across a lot of "someones" in our lifetimes. They often come as on & off situations.

Somebody who's 'the one' is there to build you, show you what a healthy and consistent relationship is like, make you a better person and cater to you in the long run. They are really your person.

Now, both may treat you the same and give you a connection/ bond that feels similar but they are different. Here are a few pointers that I believe help differentiate....

1) Clarity vs confusion - it's so simple but what's meant for you will arrive in clarity, not confusion so if you're always left wondering where you stand then that's an indicator that they're not the one.

2) On & off = off - If the bond is real, that on & off business doesn't exist because someone who's the one couldn't bare to be off with you even for a week.

3) Toxic? What's that - I promise you, that man who's always making you shed tears behind the scenes because of his actions or even his lack of actions isn't the one.

4) Respect - A man that truly loves you will treat you with the utmost respect so that name-calling business, manipulation, and nonchalant behavior shouldn't exist.

5) Still in the honeymoon stage- if he doesn't treat you with the same gentleness he treated you with when he was trying to get you he's not " the one" especially if there is a drastic change.

Things to remember about momentary people.

"Temporary people teach permanent lessons"

"Not everyone you lose in life is a loss"

"In order to control your life, you must control what you tolerate"

"Sometimes forget what you feel and remember what you deserve"

"A woman who knows what she brings to the table is not afraid of eating alone"

Lesson 4 - Mind over feelings!

Aka- Logic over emotion.

The Heart vs The Mind.

Your heart sees the good in every situation and can make you naive to the truth because It just wants to be loved. Your heart will create justifications for why your partner is acting the way they do. Lastly, your heart will allow you to tolerate things your brain knows you shouldn't but because you love that person you do it.

Your mind, on the other hand, is harsh. It can identify issues and red flags early, it knows your worth, what you deserve and how you should be treated and it sees things directly as they are without sugarcoating.

These two frequently clash because your heart will want to stay in a situation that isn't necessarily good for you because it believes there could be potential, whereas your mind understands that if someone truly loves you, they will act accordingly.

Adapting the "mind over feelings" mindset is extremely important if you want to have the upper hand because when you're able to see things directly as they are, it's easier for you to identify your position in someone's life.

Remember, actions always speak louder than words and your brain realises this but your heart will take their words and try to use them as a form of hope.

1 + 1 is 2, similar to that concept, If someone is not treating you how you want to be treated it means they don't deem you as worthy of that treatment...it's harsh but true. You have to sometimes disregard the feelings your heart feel and use your brain to spot the truth.

Men are complicated, but not as complex as we make it seem.

When a man is truly invested they will go above and beyond, so if you are finding yourself asking for the bare minimum, chances are that the situation isn't right because men will apply pressure on their own, they never need a coach. If you want the upper hand, make sure your brain is your best friend. She's harsh but she's gonna give you that raw truth every time, kinda like that one friend we all have.

Things to remember about emotional strength.

"Don't let your emotions overpower your intelligence"

"Your heart can rule your emotions but your mind
should   rule your actions"

"In order to control your life, you must control what

you tolerate"

"Sometimes forget what you feel and remember what

you deserve"

" stop trying to see the good in people and take their

actions as an answer"

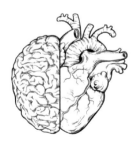

Lesson 5 - Be in control

You steer the wheel, you decide!

Control is the ability to be in charge of a situation and have an influence on an outcome.

Being in control is not the same as being controlling, the difference is that when you are in control you have an equal influence when it comes to your relationships so it's never one-sided because your expectations are always valued and taken into consideration. I've witnessed women being dragged on emotional rollercoasters because they let the man dictate everything. They let him dictate the pace of the relationship, the title, or even how often they go on dates.

Remember, this is our world, not theirs.

Gaining control can be hard for some women, it's all down to your personality but you do have to be able to stand on your expectations at all times.

How can I gain control?

The best way to gain control is to keep an ultimatum mindset, you have to be able to show people that there are certain things you won't tolerate and that there are expectations that have to be met, or else you will simply leave. Similarly to a vintage painting, you'd only give it to someone who understands and appreciates its value in order to ensure it's taken care of. Women need to use that same analogy when it comes to men by only giving men who respect them and see their value the time of day.

Men are contradicting species, they will always always respect the girl that is tough to get and has high expectations rather than the girl that will ride or die and stick beside him through his bullsh*t. Don't ever underestimate just how much power "the woman that got away" holds.

Any man will tell you, It drives them crazy with guilt when they mess things up with a good woman & she just peacefully leaves instead of making a scene & always seeking closure. That is how you gain the upper hand because you didn't even do much yet much was done.

Things to remember about control.

"Stand for nothing then you're gonna fall for

everything"

"Be the type of woman who knows what she wants and

stands by it till the end"

"You can't force someone to respect you but you can

refuse to be disrespected"

"Respect yourself enough to walk away from anyone who

doesn't respect you enough"

"Don't control him, let him do what he wants and see what

he'd rather do then there's your answer"

Lesson 6 - Me, myself and I

Ladies, Sing it!

In this life, knowing your worth is so important because if you know the weight your presence holds and the impact your company has on people, you'll find it easier to give your time to only those that deserve it. They always say the world doesn't revolve around you but surely it does since you are the main character of your story?

Most men avoid women who know their worth because it means they can't play games with you, why? Because they know you can always leave & simply find better. A woman that knows her worth understands how gentle, impactful & rare the kind of love that she has to offer is so she expects the most from anyone she gives it to.

2 things you bring to the table.

_____

_____

Beyonce said "the best revenge is your paper" so the best thing you can do for yourself is boss up, not even necessarily in terms of money but just working on yourself, creating goals for your future, and overall working towards becoming the woman you desire to be because everything else after will follow.

Also remember, time is of the essence. You don't have to waste your time with someone who's draining just because you're "comfortable" or "bored" ...instead, use that time and work on genuinely loving yourself and get yourself to a point whereby you'll always prefer your own company over anything toxic. That's strength.

That's how to have the upper hand.

Things to remember about Self love.

"Women like you don't come around often, you're rare"

"Don't dwell on what you aren't, appreciate what you are"

"You are a work of art designed by someone perfect" -

"You are more than enough, maybe people who don't see it just prefer less"

"If you're searching for someone to love you, start by looking in the mirror"

Lesson 7 - I promise you,

There's a guy that will.

I pinky promise!

Life is a game of trial and error, you win some you lose some but overall you always learn some.

I want all women to understand that what one Man won't do another will do without even being told to. By nature, men are pleasers, especially for their wives so if you ever find yourself begging or even asking for the bare minimum please do yourself a favour and go where you are appreciated.

Men have this funny "I'll only do that for my wife" mentality whereby you have to hold a special place in their hearts for them to go above and beyond. For instance, if you ask most men if they would take their one-night stands or sneaky links on a nice date most will tell you hell to the no. After speaking to all my male friends I've realised They ALL have an idea of what their "ideal" woman is like so more often than not unless you fit in the description they just won't go above and beyond for you.

They will still keep you around regardless though. However, there is a man somewhere out there that has an idea of what the perfect woman is like and you match that description to the T.

So why ever settle?

Also, the sooner you stop asking for things & literally just take their behaviour as an answer the better life will get.

The day I realised this was when I randomly remembered how my old partner could never remember my middle name or favourite colour but fast forward a year later I met someone so attentive to the point he noticed the smallest things about me for example, how my right eye gets teary when I'm nervous (i didn't even realise that myself).

But anyway, the point I'm trying to make is...what one won't do, another will, just wait and see.

<u>Reminders about finding the right person.</u>

"Some men won't know what your favorite flowers are and will simply leave it as that but another will take you to the florist and see which ones make your smile light up the most to find out the answer" -

"What God has in store for you will be worth the wait"

"One day the ex will realise how lucky he was but by then you'll be married to someone who will never need to be reminded"

"What you're seeking is seeking you too"

"One day someone will walk into your life and make you grateful that it didn't work out with your previous situations"

41

The Upperhand is all about you.

What <u>YOU</u> tolerate.

How <u>YOU</u> view yourself.

Who <u>YOU</u> allow to have access to you.

Where <u>YOU</u> see yourself in a few years.

When <u>YOU</u> decide enough is enough.

Let the self development

start...

1) A woman with the upper hand doesn't do much compromising, she stands by her beliefs and she'd rather stand alone strong and wait for a situation that brings her peace than just accept whatever's given to her.

- What are the top 5 things you promise yourself to never tolerate?

Remember these and if you find yourself in a situation whereby your partner does even ⅕ of these then just know you're settling.

2) A woman with the upper hand prioritises herself first. She's got her goals, her future, and her own dreams to chase before she thinks about investing in a relationship.

Goals you want to achieve within the next 6 months...

Goals you want to achieve mentally...

Goals you want to achieve within the next 5 years...

Career Goals...

Body goals...

| |
| |
| |

3) A woman with the upper hand is accountable. We all have flaws, toxic traits, and negative responses from childhood trauma. Identifying them & understanding the impact they may have on your relationships is important.

-What are some traits about yourself that you consider negative or toxic?

Your flaws / toxic traits	Has it affected a relationship or friendship?

4) A woman with the upper hand has an idea of the "dream woman" she aspires to be one day and she takes baby steps to slowly work on becoming her. You are your dream woman, make that little girl you used to be proud.

-Describe in detail what your idea of the dream woman is.

_____

_____

_____

_____

_____

loading...

5) A woman with the upper hand is grateful. She's appreciative of the lessons she's learnt, her growth as a person and she's excited for what's yet to come.

What are some things that you are grateful for?

*

*

*

*

*

*

6) A woman with the upper hand is secure in herself, she knows her worth. She understands that she brings a lot to the table and therefore she only gives her time to those deserving of it.

What are a few things you really love about yourself?

7) A woman with the upperhand knows what she wants in a partner. She may not know how he will look but she definitely knows how she wants him to treat her.

What do you expect from your partner? Focus on how you want to be treated rather than looks/ personality.

_____

_____

_____

_____

_____

_____

keep watering yourself, your're growing,

make peace with the broken pieces

know your worth & add tax

it's your world, hire and fire accordingly.

Self love = Secret to happiness

Don't let anyones son tek you fi ediaat

Become MRS standing on business.

Notes

Notes

To everyone who made it to the end, I'd like to

say thank you from the bottom of my heart.

Thank you

Merci

Gracias

E dupe

Ngiyabonga

Dedicated to Onias Claver Masiwa.

Q&A about the author.

<u>Q-what sparked your interest in writing a self-help book?</u>

<u>A</u>-Growing up, I lived half my life with my grandparents in Zimbabwe, where I witnessed their healthy, kind, patient, and admirable relationship. I got to see the meaning of soft love. Fast forward to mid-primary school, I moved to a single-parent household in London, the dynamics were quite opposite in terms of my parent's relationship compared to what I was used to.

This contrast sparked curiosity within me and made me curious to understand why relationships can be so different and what I need to do to assure I'm in the healthiest relationship.

<u>Q- what are your aims with this book?</u>

A- Sounds cliche but honestly, if I can help someone to genuinely want better for themselves after reading this book, I've won and I'm happy.

<u>Q- who are you?</u>

A - A girl from north London.

Made in the USA
Middletown, DE
29 May 2024

55014971R00040